Margaret Fuller, Caroline Wells Healey Dall

Margaret and Her Friends; or, Ten Conversations with Margaret Fuller

Upon the Mythology of the Greeks and its Expression in Art

Margaret Fuller, Caroline Wells Healey Dall

Margaret and Her Friends; or, Ten Conversations with Margaret Fuller
Upon the Mythology of the Greeks and its Expression in Art

ISBN/EAN: 9783337191184

Printed in Europe, USA, Canada, Australia, Japan

Cover: Foto ©Thomas Meinert / pixelio.de

More available books at **www.hansebooks.com**

MARGARET AND HER FRIENDS

MARGARET AND HER FRIENDS

OR

𝕿en 𝕮onversations

WITH

MARGARET FULLER

UPON

THE MYTHOLOGY OF THE GREEKS AND ITS EXPRESSION IN ART

HELD AT THE HOUSE OF THE REV. GEORGE RIPLEY
BEDFORD PLACE, BOSTON

BEGINNING MARCH 1, 1841

REPORTED BY CAROLINE W. HEALEY

BOSTON

ROBERTS BROTHERS

1895

University Press:
JOHN WILSON AND SON, CAMBRIDGE, U. S. A.

TABLE OF CONTENTS.

———◆———

[1] Emerson's presence at Conversations II. V. and VIII. is noted above, because in his contribution to Margaret's "Memoirs" he shows that his attendance made absolutely no impression on him. He states that there were but *five* Conversations, and that he was present only at the second.

PREFACE.

IN 1839, Margaret Fuller, delicate in health and much overtaxed, consented to gratify many who loved her by opening in Boston a series of " Conversations for Women." In a Circular quoted by Emerson, she says to Mrs. Sophia Ripley : —

" Could a circle be assembled in earnest, desirous to answer the questions, ' What were we born to do ? ' and ' How shall we do it ? ' I should think the undertaking a noble one."

This was certainly the original intent of the famous " Fuller Conversations," which, beginning then, were continued at

intervals, until Margaret left Boston for
New York in 1844.

It seems a little singular, therefore, to
find her writing to Ralph Waldo Emerson of this series, Nov. 25, 1839, as
follows : —

"The first day's topic was the genealogy
of Heaven and Earth; then the Will or
Jupiter; the Understanding, Mercury: the
second day's, The celestial inspiration of
Genius, perception and transmission of Divine
Law; Apollo the terrene inspiration, Bacchus
the impassioned abandonment. Of the thun-
derbolt, the caduceus, the ray and the grape,
having disposed as well as might be, we came
to the wave and the sea-shell it moulds to
beauty. . . .

"I assure you, there is more Greek than
Bostonian spoken at the meetings!"

Under the forms suggested by Mythology, Margaret proceeded to open all
the great questions of life. In a literary
sense, she distinctly stated that she knew

little about the doings on Olympus, nor had she received any help from German critical works, — of which at the present day she would have found many.

These Conversations owed their attraction first to the absolute novelty of her theme to many of those she addressed, and still more to the variety and freshness of her own treatment. The opening, at the Boston Athenæum, of the splendid collection of casts presented by Thomas Handasyd Perkins, and many private collections of pictures, engravings, gems, and miniature casts, had interested her intensely, and both mind and fancy were absorbed in the contemplation of their themes. In these Conversations she depicted what she had gained from Art, rather than the little that she had acquired through study. If I may judge from a later experience, her Latin studies rather injured than developed her

brilliant fancies.   She never could remember what she had said, never could
repeat a brilliant saying, and, if obliged
to read any illustration, read it, as all her
friends admitted, very badly.   From a
statement made to Emerson, I quote the
following : —

" Her mood applied itself to the mood of her
companion, point to point, in the most limber,
sinuous, vital way ; . . . and this sympathy
she had for all persons indifferently."

The communication of which the above
is a sample I have always read with
amazement, for I never knew a person
of whom it would seem less true.   When
conversing with one sympathetic person,
it was undoubtedly true ; when resting
upon the affection and loyalty of her
young women, — a most gifted and ex-
traordinary circle, — it was doubtless
equally so ; but when the class of March,

1841, was formed, a very different aspect of herself appeared.

The fame of her "talks" had spread. She had great need of money, and some of the gentlemen who were accustomed to talk with her, and some of the ladies of her day-class, suggested an evening class, to be composed of both ladies and gentlemen, and to meet at the house of the Rev. George Ripley in Bedford Place. Ten Conversations were to be held, and the tickets of admission cost twenty dollars each, a very high price for that time. It was in the book-room of Elisabeth Peabody that I first heard them discussed. I was very young to join such a circle; and when she invited me, Elisabeth had more regard, I think, to Margaret's purse, than to my fitness for the company. But it was a great opportunity. The members were full of excitement over the projected opening of

Brook Farm. All were in good spirits, and bright sayings ran back and forth. I had been carefully trained in the Art of Reporting, and at that time made careful abstracts on the following day of any lecture that had interested me. In these I trusted to my memory. It was not possible to do this with the Conversations; so I invented a sort of shorthand, and carried note-book and pencil with me. I sat a little out of sight that I might not embarrass Margaret, but Elisabeth Peabody and Mrs. Farrar found me out. Elisabeth wrote what she called an abstract, every night; but an examination of her abstracts quoted by Mr. Emerson shows that what she wrote was not what any one said, but the impression made upon her own mind by it. These abstracts she always read to me, the next morning. I wrote out my short-hand notes before breakfast and carried them

down to her about noon. I greatly enjoyed listening to her papers, and she
was so absorbed in them that she often
forgot to ask for mine, which was a great
relief to me.

So far as I know, these Reports of
mine are the only attempt ever made
deliberately to represent these or any
of Margaret's " Conversations " word for
word. Of course, much was omitted as
not worth recording, nor did I ever write
down anything that I could not understand. Many of the members I knew
intimately, and fell naturally into writing of them by initials and first names,
as they always spoke to and of each
other. At times I fell back into the
Mr., Mrs., or Miss, which was my own
habit. It is well to call those we love
by any name they will permit, but the
familiar habit of the Transcendental
circle was full of social peril to the

younger members, who, conceiving it a
proof of genius, followed it, when its
origin was forgotten, and were much
misunderstood in consequence in later
years.

I offer the Reports exactly as they
were written. I should like to alter
them in several small ways if I could do
it honestly. We met to discuss Grecian
Mythology as interpreted to Margaret's
mind by Art; but Latin and Greek names
were used as if they were synonymous,
and Latin poems were quoted, as well as
Greek traditions. This confused my
mind then, and does still. Athene and
Minerva, Zeus and Jupiter, are by no
means the same persons to me, Art or
no Art.

It may be thought by those who cannot remember the persons who enacted
this little drama, or by those who do
remember and know well how very dis-

tinguished a company this was, that I should have eliminated my own reflections, and dropped out of the story.

This would I think have been greatly unjust to Margaret, who never enjoyed this mixed class, and considered it a failure so far as her own power was concerned. She and Mr. Emerson met like Pyramus and Thisbe, a blank wall between. With Mr. Alcott she had no patience, and no one of the class seemed to understand how sincere and deep was her interest in the theme. In no way was Margaret's supremacy so evident as in the impulse she gave to the minds of younger women.

It was the wish of Margaret's mother and brothers, as it is also the wish of her surviving relatives, that I should print these pages. After Arthur's death, Richard Fuller undertook to carry out a plan to which both had agreed, and

which Margaret's mother had greatly at
heart. They desired that I should write
a simple, straightforward account of Margaret, including her residence in Italy,
her marriage, the birth of her child, and
her death. This they intended to print
at their own expense, and they thought
it might be so written as to put an end to
many absurd and painful rumors which
had followed the publication of the first
Memoir. That I might prepare for this,
all Margaret's manuscripts were in my
custody for more than a year. The
completion of the work was prevented
by Richard Fuller's unexpected death.
No surviving member of the family was
able to carry out his intention.

I still have in my possession the esti-
mate of his sister's character which
Richard made for my use.

I should like to add, that the scholar
will see that the stories from Apuleius

and Novalis do not exactly correspond to the originals. They were reported exactly as they were told.

CAROLINE HEALEY DALL.

Sept. 1, 1895,
WASHINGTON, D. C.

A LIST OF PERSONS

ATTENDING

THE CLASS NAMED IN THIS REPORT.

About thirty persons usually attended.

———

GEORGE RIPLEY. The well-known clergy-man, settled over a Unitarian church in Purchase St., Boston, afterward the President of the Association at Brook Farm, and later literary editor of the New York "Tribune."

SOPHIA DANA RIPLEY, his wife.

ELISABETH PALMER PEABODY. A woman of remarkable accumulations of learning, and as remarkable a breadth of sympathy. She was a teacher,— an enthusiastic advocate of the Kindergarten, and opened at No. 13 West St., Boston, a foreign Circulating Library, which soon became a sort of Literary Exchange of the greatest use to New England. Her own great powers did not accomplish all they ought, because it was impossible for her to apply them systematically.

FREDERICK HENRY HEDGE. The well-known German and ecclesiastical scholar, whose remarkable scholarship and character have not yet received the commemoration they deserve. He was at this time settled over the church in Bangor, Maine.

JAMES FREEMAN CLARKE. Already the pastor of the Church of the Disciples, in Boston, and preaching at Amory Hall. The outline of his lovely and useful life is preserved in a memoir by the Rev. E. E. Hale, D.D.

RALPH WALDO EMERSON. The Concord philosopher.

MRS. FARRAR, born Rotch, the wife of the Harvard Professor of Physical Science and Mathematics.

FRANCIS G. SHAW. The son of a well-known Boston merchant, to be honored through all time as the father of Colonel Robert G. Shaw, who was buried where he fell, with the negroes whom he died to free.

Mrs. Sarah B. Shaw, his wife.

Ann Wilby Clarke, wife of a Boston bank-officer and the oldest member of an English family of Wilbys, nearly every member of which was at some time a teacher in Boston or its neighborhood.

Mrs. Jonathan Russell of Milton, widow of the U. S. Minister to Sweden (1814–1818), residing on the old Governor Hutchinson place at Milton, and

Miss Ida Russell, her daughter.

William White. The brother of the first wife of James Russell Lowell, who was killed by a fall from the bluff at Milwaukee in 1856.

William W. Story. Sculptor, poet, and lawyer, and well known as a contributor to Blackwood. Still living.

Caroline Sturgis, daughter of William Sturgis of Boston, — married later to Mr. Tappan, — a most gifted and charming creature.

Mrs. Anna Barker Ward, wife of S. G. Ward, now living in Washington.

Jones Very of Salem. A Transcendental poet.

ELISABETH HOAR was the daughter of Samuel Hoar of Concord, Mass., and of Sarah, the daughter of Roger Sherman of Connecticut. Elisabeth was not the least gifted of her very gifted family. One brother, recently deceased, was President Grant's first Attorney-General; another is the well-known Senator from Massachusetts to the Congress of the United States; and a third, Edward Sherman Hoar, was distinguished as a scholar and botanist. To great intellectual gifts, Elisabeth added personal loveliness and a saintly serenity of character. She was betrothed to Charles Emerson (a brother of Ralph Waldo Emerson), who died of sudden illness just before the time appointed for their marriage. He was also a rarely gifted person, and after his death his family transferred their tenderest affection to Elisabeth. The reader of the various Lives of Emerson will see that she is often mentioned, and several of Emerson's letters are addressed to her. Had she chosen to devote herself to literature, she would have been greatly distinguished. The Life of Mrs. Ripley of Waltham, written for " The Women of Our First Century," and published by a committee appointed at the Centennial Exhibition in Philadelphia, was written by her. She died in 1878.

A. Bronson Alcott of Concord. A memoir of him has been written by the Hon. F. B. Sanborn of Concord, assisted by Wm. T. Harris.

W. Mack. A gentleman of great ability, who taught a school in Belmont. His daughter was the first wife of Stillman, the artist. The family is, I think, extinct, unless Mrs. Stillman left a daughter.

Sophia Peabody. A younger sister of E. P. P., afterwards Mrs. Nathaniel Hawthorne.

Marianne Jackson. A lovely, beloved, and accomplished woman, who died early. She was the daughter of Judge Charles Jackson, one of the soundest jurists who ever sat on a Massachusetts bench, — the sister of Mrs. Oliver Wendell Holmes, of Mrs. Charles C. Paine, and the aunt, I believe, of Mr. John T. Morse.

I have reserved for the last the name of the only sound Greek scholar among us: Charles Wheeler.

CHARLES STEARNS WHEELER. Born in Lincoln, near Concord, Dec. 19, 1816, of H. U. 1837, distinguished as a Greek scholar from whom much was expected. To economize in order to pursue his Greek studies he built a shanty at Walden, which is said to have served as a suggestion to Thoreau. He went to Germany directly after these Conversations, and died suddenly of fever at Leipzig, in the summer of 1843. His death was a great grief and a great shock. I have not forgotten the sensation it produced. Beloved and honored by all who knew him, the community of scholars was especially bereaved. To this day, I am able to trust fearlessly to any information obtained from him.

" Only a signal shown, and a distant voice in the darkness." — LONGFELLOW.

MARGARET AND HER FRIENDS.

I.

MARGARET opened the conversation by a beautiful sketch of the origin of Mythology. The Greeks she thought borrowed their Gods from the Hindus and Egyptians, but they idealized their personifications to a far greater extent. The Hindus dwelt in the All, the Infinite, which the Greeks analyzed and to some degree humanized. All things sprang from Cœlus and Terra., — that is, from Heaven and Earth, or spirit and matter. Rhea, or the Productive Energy, and Saturn, or Time, were the children of Cœlus and Terra. The progress of any people is marked by its mythi. Mythology is only the history of the development of the Infinite in the Finite. Saturn devoured his own children until the disappointed Rhea put a stone (or obstacle) in his way, and she succeeded in raising Jupiter. The development of human faculties was slow, therefore Time seemed to absorb all that Productive Energy brought forth, until Energy itself created obstacles; and of these was born the Indomitable Will. Jupiter represented that Will, and usurped the rule of Time, fighting with the low and sensual passions, represented by the Titans and the Giants, until he seated himself securely on the Olympian Throne, the Father of the Gods. This Will was not in itself the highest development of either Beauty, Genius, Wisdom, or Thought; but such developments were subject to it, were its children.

Juno is only the feminine form of this Indomitable Will. By herself she is inferior to it, and whenever she opposes it, loses the game. Vulcan, her child, is Mechanic Art, great in itself to be sure, but not comparable to the Perfect Wisdom, or Minerva, which sprang ready armed from the masculine Will. *She* was greater than her Father, but still his child.

Neptune, who raises always a " placid head above the waves," represents the flow of thought, — all-embracing, girdling in the world, Diana and Apollo, or Purity and Genius.

Mercury is Genius in the extrinsic, of eloquence, human understanding, and expression. All were the embodiments of Absolute Ideas, of ideas that had no origin, — that were eternal. Love brooded over Chaos; and the perfect Beauty and Love, represented among the

Greeks by Venus and her son, rose from the turbid elements. It is singular that even the ancients should have maintained the pre-existence of Love. It was before Order, Men, or the Gods men worshipped. The fable suggests the truth, — Infinite Love and Beauty always was. It is only with their development in finite beings that History has to do.

Here MARGARET recapitulated. The Indomitable Will had dethroned Time, and, acting with Productive Energy, — variously represented at different times by Isis, Rhea, Ceres, Persephone, and so on, — had driven back the sensual passions to the bowels of the earth, while it produced Perfect Wisdom, Genius, Beauty, and Love, results which were more excellent if not more powerful than their Cause.

To understand this Mythology, we must denationalize ourselves, and throw the mind back to the consideration of Greek Art, Literature, and Poesy. It is only scanty justice that my pen can render to Margaret's eloquent talk.

FRANK SHAW asked her how she imagined these personifications to have suggested themselves in that barbarous age.

MARGARET objected to the word *barbarous*. She believed that in the age of Plato the human intellect reached a point as elevated in some respects as any it had ever touched.

But the Gods were not the product of that age, but of another far more remote, FRANK objected. Was not the infinity of Hindu conception impaired, when the Greeks attributed to the Gods the duties, passions, and criminal indulgences of men?

MRS. RIPLEY said that the virtue of the Hindu lay in contemplation. If a man had seen *God*, he was exempt from the ordinary obligations of life, and allowed to pass his life in quiet adoration.

MARGARET added that the Greek knew better than that. *He* felt the necessity of developing the Infinite through action, and embodied this necessity in his art and poesy as well as in his myths.

FRANK seemed still to think that in losing the adoring contemplation of the Hindu, and bringing their deities to the human level, the Greeks had taken one step down.

E. P. P. had always thought it had been a step *up*, and ANN CLARKE thought that the Greeks forgot themselves, merged all remembrance of the Finite, in realizing the individual forces of the Infinite.

WILLIAM WHITE, who had not waded very far into the stream, thought the North American Indian's worship of the

Manitou purer than the Greek worship, for the very reason that the Indian ascribed to his Manitou no passion that had degraded humanity.

MARGARET said that the Indian propitiated his God by vile deeds, by ignoble treacheries and revenge. So the Hindu throws her child into the Ganges, and an ecstatic crowd falls before the car of Juggernaut.

I thought a good deal, but did not speak. Did not William's question grow out of the simple Unity of the Indian worship? But the Indian does not worship the Manitou because he recognizes a single First Cause, comprehending in itself all beauty, wisdom, purity, and truth, but because his heart is naturally lifted toward an unknown something, which he has hardly yet considered as a Cause. The Greek recognized the abstract forces of the Universe, but did not perceive their Unity, and so personified them separately.

E. P. P. suggested that the Indian had no literature, and had left no record of his Olympus!

MARGARET added that, if we compare the Indian Elysium with the Greek, the difference in spirituality is perceived at once.

HENRY HEDGE said that Frank Shaw talked about Greek mythi, but nobody could show a purely Greek mythos.

FRANK replied that he only meant that when the Greek mind had acted on a myth, it had not refined it.

MARGARET added that it was a vulgar notion that the Poets of Greece created her Gods; that the Poets were objective, and could give only humanized representations of them.

HENRY HEDGE thought that there was a point to which philosophy aided and prompted the creative power, but, that point passed, rather checked its action. Analysis took the place of the objective tendency.

Well! said WILLIAM WHITE, would not the human mind, aided only by culture, be incapable of any better idea than Frank Shaw suggested? Must not revelation complete the work?

MARGARET said that the answer to his question would be determined by his understanding of the word " revelation." *She* could not believe in a God who had ever left himself without a witness in the world. As soon as the human mind and will were ready, there was always some great Truth waiting to be submitted to their united action, until it was worn out. The beautiful Greek era had been succeeded by a period of inaction; the Roman era by another, and so on. She was sorry we had wandered from our subject so far as to doubt her very premises!

FRANK said, everything rested on those premises; so he thought that the ideals of beauty, love, justice, and truth should be referred to the Infinite Mind, and not to the Greek.

I wonder where he was when Margaret told about the Love which "was" before Order!

HENRY HEDGE said that Culture was the Mediator between the Finite and the Infinite.

JAMES FREEMAN CLARKE, alluding to Mr. Hedge's previous remark upon the growth of philosophy, and the loss of the creative power, said that if that were a fact, it greatly diminished the probability of the birth of pure Genius into the world. Plato wrote when philosophy was at the turning point.

MARGARET said that there were many

proofs in Plato that the philosophers understood the personifications of the mythi. She thought that the gods, the demigods, and the heroes of mythology represented distinct classes, and that this was not sufficiently remembered. She referred to the story of the burning of Hercules in Ovid, where Jupiter calls Juno to see how well his son endures!

WILLIAM WHITE said that he thought the idea of Deity was degraded when the Greeks changed a hero into a god; but if Culture be a Mediator, would not Plato have been greater had he been born into the nineteenth century?

JAMES F. CLARKE said Platos were impossible now.

MARGARET agreed, and said that the pride of knowledge which he would find in the world should he appear, would be a greater obstacle than superstition once was.

Did somebody say a little while ago that Will indomitable was born of obstacle?

MARGARET told William White that Coleridge had once said that he could neither measure nor understand Plato's ignorance! His mind had not reached that altitude!

HENRY HEDGE, not willing to forego the possible birth of Genius, asked if all the experience and discovery with which the world had been enriched since Plato's time would not furnish enough for the new-comer to act upon?

MARGARET replied that the mind could not receive unless excited. She must go through all the intellectual experience of a Plato, to be as great as he; but she might stand upon the general or even her own intuitive recognition of the truths he had advanced, and go forward to greater results, — but still that would not be to make herself greater.

But, said MRS. RIPLEY, in the first case you would be nothing *but* Plato.

MARGARET acceded, but begged not to be understood as doubting that the future would be capable of finer things than the past.

The ideal significance of the Mythology was further dwelt upon, and much was said of the contrast between the thought of the priest and the worship of the people. It was acknowledged as a matter of course, that only a few preserved any consciousness of the original significance of the Mythology.

HENRY HEDGE thought that this was the true key to the purpose of the Eleusinian mysteries, whether in Egypt where they originated, or in Greece where they were introduced. Through them, all who chose became initiated into the interior meaning of the Mythology.

CHARLES WHEELER added, that in

the flourishing times of the Athenian Republic every citizen was compelled to initiate himself.

MARGARET closed our talk with a gentle reproof to our wandering wits. To prevent such desultory prattling, she desired that a subject should be proposed for the next evening. The story of Ceres or Rhea, in fact the Productive Energy however manifested, carried general favor, and Margaret said archly that she had thought the presence of gentlemen (who had never until now attended one of her talks) would prevent the wandering and keep us free from prejudice!

I thought she was rightly disappointed.

I cannot recall the words, but at some time this evening Margaret distinguished three mythological dynasties. The first was the reign of the Natural Powers. The second, represented by Jupiter,

Pluto, and Neptune, stood for the height, the depth, and the surface or flow of things, the first manifestations of human consciousness. The third was the Bacchic, Bacchus not being yet, in her estimation, the vulgar God of the wine-vat and the festival, but the inspired Genius, — being to Apollo, as she said, what the nectar is to the grape.

CAROLINE W. HEALEY.

March 2, 1841.

II.

MARGARET recapitulated the statements she made last week. By thus giving to each fabled Deity its place in the scheme of Mythology, she did not mean to ignore the enfolding ideas, the one thought developed in all — as in Rhea, Bacchus, Pan. She would only imply that each personification was individual, served a particular purpose, and was worshipped in a particular way.

Before proceeding to talk about Ceres, she wished to remind us of the mischief of wandering from our subject. She hoped the ground she offered would be accepted *at least to talk about!* Certainly no one could deny that a mythos was the last and best growth of a national

mind, and that in this case the charac-
teristics of the Greek mind were best
gathered from this creation.

Ceres, Persephone, and Isis, as well as
Rhea, Diana, and so on, seem to be only
modifications of one enfolding idea, — a
goddess accepted by all nations, and not
peculiar to Greece. The pilgrimages of
the more prominent of these goddesses,
Ceres and Isis, seem to indicate the
life which loses what is dear in childhood, to seek in weary pain for what
after all can be but half regained. Ceres
regained her daughter, but only for half
the year. Isis found her husband, but
dismembered. This era in Mythology
seems to mark the progress of a people
from an unconscious to a conscious state.
Persephone's periodical exile shows the
impossibility of resuming an unconscious-
ness from which we have been once
aroused, the need thought has, having

once felt the influence of the Seasons, to retire into itself.

CHARLES WHEELER reminded Margaret that she had said that the predominant goddesses, without reference to Greece, enfolded only one idea, that of the female *Will* or *Genius*, — *the bounteous giver.* He had asked her if she could sustain herself by etymological facts, and she replied that her knowledge of the Greek was not critical enough. Since then he had inquired into the origin of the proper names of the Greek deities, and found that it confirmed her impression. The names of Rhea, Tellus, Isis, and Diana were resolvable into one, and the difference in their etymology was only a common and permissible change in the position of the letters of which they are composed, or a mere provincial dialectic change. Diana is the same as Dione, also one of the names of Juno.

E. P. P. asked if Homer ever con-founded the last two? MARGARET thought not. Homer was purely objec-tive. He knew little and cared less about the primitive creation of the myths.

R. W. EMERSON thought it would be very difficult to detect this secret. Ju-piter, for instance, might have been a man who was the exponent of Will to his race.

MARGARET said, " No; they could have deduced him just as easily from Nature herself, or from a single exhibition of will power."

R. W. EMERSON said that a man like Napoleon would easily have sug-gested it.

" What a God-send is a Napoleon!" exclaimed CHARLES WHEELER; "let us pray for scores of such, that a new and superior mythos may arise for us!" Is it malicious to suspect a subtle irony turned against the sacred person of R. W. E. in this speech?

MARGARET retorted indignantly that if they came, *we* should do nothing better than write memoirs of their hats, coats, and swords, as we had done already, without thinking of any lesson they might teach. She could not see why we were not content to take the beautiful Greek mythi as they were, without troubling ourselves about those which might arise for us!

R. W. E. acknowledged that the Greeks had a quicker perception of the beautiful than we. Their genius lay in the material expression of it. If we knew the real meaning of the names of their Deities, the story would take to flight. We should have only the working of abstract ideas as we might adjust them for ourselves.

MARGARET said that a fable was more than a mere word. It was a word of the purest kind rather, the passing of thought into form. R. W. E. had made no allowance for time or space or climate, and there was a want of truth in that. The age of the Greeks was the age of Poetry; ours was the age of Analysis. *We* could not create a Mythology.

EMERSON asked, " Why not? We had still better material."

MARGARET said, irrelevantly as it seemed to me, that Carlyle had attempted to deduce new principles from present history, and that was the reason he did not *respect* the *respectable.*

EMERSON said Carlyle was unfortunate in his figures, but we might have mythology as beautiful as the Greek.

MARGARET thought each age of the world had its own work to do. The transition of thought into form marked the Greek period. It was most easily done through fable, on account of their intense perception of beauty.

EMERSON pursued his own train of thought. He seemed to forget that we had come together to pursue Margaret's. He said it was impossible that men or events should *stand out* in a population of twenty millions as they could from a population of a single million, to which the whole population of the ancient world could hardly have amounted. As Hercules stood to Greece, no modern man could ever stand in relation to his own world.

MARGARET thought Hercules and Jupiter quite different creations. The first *might* have been a deified life. The second could not.

CHARLES WHEELER said that R. W. E.'s view carried no historical obligation of belief with it. We could not deny the heroic origin of the Greek demi-gods, but the highest dynasty was the exponent of translated thought.

Sophia Ripley asked if the life of an individual fitly interwoven with her experience was not as fine a Poem as the story of Ceres, her wanderings and her tears? Did not Margaret know such lives?

R. W. E. thought every man had probably met his Jupiter, Juno, Minerva, Venus, or Ceres in society!

Margaret was sure she never had!

R. W. E. explained: "Not in the world, but each on his own platform."

William Story objected. The life of an individual was not univer-sal. (!)

Sophia Ripley repeated, "The inner life."

William Story claimed to be an in-dividual, and did not think individual experience could ever meet all minds, — like the story of Ceres, for example.

Sophia said all experience was universal.

I said nothing, but held this colloquy with myself. Thought is the best of human nature; its fulness urges expression: its need of being met, not only by *one* other but by every other, *craves* it. This craving is the acknowledgment of the universal experience. What is *purely* individual is perishable. *Identity* is to be separated from individuality for this cause.

Margaret said the element of beauty would be wanting to our creations. A fine emotion glowed through features which seem to fall like a soft veil over the soul, while it could scarce do more than animate those that were obtuse and coarse in every outline. (!)

" Then," said William Story, and

my heart thanked the *preux chevalier*, —
" then something is wanting in the
emotion itself."

WILLIAM WHITE said, stupidly, that
sunlight could not fall with equal charm
on rocks and the green grass. (!)

I asked if the rock could not give
what it did not receive ?   Flung back by
rugged points and relieved by dark
shadows, was not the sunlight itself
transfigured ?

STORY said every face had its own
beauty.   No act that was natural could
be ungraceful.

EMERSON said that we all did sundry
graceful acts, in our caps and tunics,
which we never could do again, which
we never wanted to do again.

MARGARET said, at last we had touched
the point.   We could not restore the
childhood of the world, but could we not
admire this simple plastic period, and

4

gather from it some notion of the Greek genius?

R. W. E. thought this legitimate. He would have it that we could not determine the origin of a mythos, but we might fulfil Miss Fuller's intention.

MARGARET said history reconciled us to life, by showing that man had redeemed himself. Genius needed that encouragement.

Not *Genius*, SOPHIA RIPLEY thought; common natures needed it, but Genius was self-supported.

MARGARET said it might be the consolation of Genius.

MRS. RUSSELL asked why Miss Fuller found so much fault with the present.

MARGARET *had* no fault to find with it. She took facts as they were. Every age did something toward fulfilling the cycle of mind. The work of the Greeks was not ours.

SOPHIA RIPLEY asked if the mythology
had been a prophecy of the Greek mind
to itself, or if the nation had experienced
life in any wide or deep sense.

MARGARET seemed a little out of
patience, and no wonder! She said it
did not matter which. The question
was, what could *we find* in the mythi,
and what did the Greeks mean that we
should find there. Coleridge once said
that certain people were continually saying of Shakespeare, that he did not mean
to impart certain spiritual meanings to
some of his sketches of life and character ; but if Shakespeare did not mean it
his Genius did: so if the Greeks meant not
this or that, the Greek genius meant it.

In relation to the progress of the ages,
JAMES F. CLARKE said that the story of
Persephone concealed in the bowels of
the earth for half the year seemed to
him to indicate something of their com-

parative states. Persephone was the seed which must return to earth before it could fructify. Thought must retire into itself before it can be regenerate.

MARGARET was pleased with this, more especially as in the story of the Goddess it is eating the pomegranate, whose seed is longest in germinating, which dooms her to the realm of Pluto.

GEORGE RIPLEY remarked that we saw this need of withdrawal in the slothful ages when mind seemed to be imbibing energy for future action. The world sometimes forsook a quest and returned to it. We had forsaken Beauty, but we might return to it.

Certainly, MARGARET assented. A perfect mind would detect all beauty in the hearth-rug at her feet: the meanest part of creation contained the whole; but the labor we were now at to appreciate the Greek proved conclusively that *we* were not Greek. A simple plastic nature would take it all in with delight, without doubt or question.

Or rather, amended EMERSON, would take it up and go forward with it.

It makes no difference, said MARGARET, for we live in a circle.

I did not think it pleasant to track and retrack the same arc, and preferred to go forward with R. W. E., so I asked if there was to be no *higher* poetry.

MARGARET acknowledged that there was something beyond the aspiration of the Egyptian or the poetry of the Greek.

GEORGE RIPLEY thought we had not lost all reverence for these abstract forces. The Eleusinian mysteries might be forgotten, but not Ceres. We did not worship in ignorance. The mysteries led back to the Infinite. The processes of vegetation were actually heart-rending!

Here, *I* thought, was a basis for my higher poetry.

GEORGE RIPLEY acknowledged that it was so. He seemed to be more conscious of the movement of the world than any of our party. He said we must not measure creation by Boston and Washington, as we were too apt to do. There was still France, Germany, and Prussia, — perhaps Russia! The work of this generation was not religious nor poetic; still, there was a tendency to go back to both. There were to be ultraisms, but also, he hoped, consistent development

CHARLES WHEELER then related the story of Isis, of her hovering in the form of a swallow round the tree in which the sarcophagus of Osiris had been enclosed by Typhon; of her being allowed to fell the tree; of the odor emitted by the royal maidens whom she touched, which revealed her Divinity to the

Queen; of the second loss of the body, as she returned home, and its final dismemberment.

There was little success in spiritualizing more of this story than the pilgrimage, and R. W. E. seemed to feel this; for when MARGARET had remarked that even a divine force must become as the birds of the air to compass its ends, and that it was in the carelessness of conscious success that the second loss occurred, he said that it was impossible to detect an inner sense in all these stories.

MARGARET replied, that she had not attempted that, but she could see it in all the prominent points.

CHARLES WHEELER said that the varieties of anecdote proved that the stories were not all authentic. It was an ancient custom to strike off medals in honor of certain acts of the Gods. To these graven pictures the common people gave their own vulgar interpretations, as they did also to the bas-reliefs on their temples and monuments.

E. P. P. said this accounted for many of the stories transmitted by Homer. When sculpture and architecture had lost their meaning, his inventive genius was only the more stimulated to find one.

CHARLES WHEELER asked what Margaret would make of the story that the tears of Isis frightened children to death?

There was a general laugh, but MARGARET said coolly, that children always shrank from a baffled hope.

Some one contrasted Persephone with her mother.

MARGARET assented to whatever was said, and added that she had been particularly struck with it in an engraving she had recently seen, in which Ceres

stood with lifted eyes, full-eyed, ma-
tronly, bounteous, ready to give all to
all, while Persephone, dejected and
thoughtful, sat meditating; and the idea
was strengthened by her discovering
that Persephone was the same as Ariadne
the deserted. I could only guess at the
remark by Margaret's comment. It
seemed to imply baffled hope for
Persephone.

The Eleusinian mysteries were now
alluded to. Although it has been said
that only moral precepts were inculcated
through these, WHEELER urged that a
whole school of Continental authors now
acknowledged that the higher doctrines
of philosophy were taught.

R. W. E. added, that as initiation became more easy such instruction must
have degenerated into a mere matter of
form, and many of the *un*initiated sur-
pass the initiated in wisdom.

MARGARET admitted this. Socrates was one of the uninitiated. The crowd seldom felt the full force of beauty in Art or Literature. To prove it, it was only necessary to walk once through the Hall of Sculpture at the Athenæum, and catch the remarks of any half-dozen on Michael Angelo's " Day and Night." He would be fortunate who heard a single observer comment on its power.

MRS. RUSSELL asked why the images of the sun and moon were introduced into these mysterious celebrations.

MARGARET asked impatiently why they had always been invoked by every child who could string two rhymes together.

I said that if Ceres was the simple *agricultural* productive energy, of course the sun was her first minister, its genial influence being as manifest as the energy itself.

In regard to the etymology of the proper names, it seemed reasonable to me that this energy should have gained attributes as it did names. Any nation devoted to the chase would learn to call the lunar deity Diana; any devoted to the cultivation of grain would project her as Ceres. The reproductive powers of flocks and herds would suggest Rhea or Juno, and philosophy or art would invoke Persephone.

When we were talking about beauty, J. F. C. quoted Goethe, and said that the spirit sometimes made a mistake and clothed itself in the wrong garment.

C. W. HEALEY.

March 9, 1841.

III.

THE third conversation was delayed by Margaret's illness, and finally took place —

March 19, 1841.

MARGARET again complained that we wandered from the subject, and told the following story from Novalis.

Imagine a room, on one side of it Eros and Fable at play. On the other, before a marble slab on which rests a vase of pure water, sits a fair woman named Sophia. Her head rests upon her hand. Between her and the children sits a man of reverend age, before a table at which he writes whatever has been or is. This is History; and as he finishes each sheet he hands it to Sophia, who dips it in the

vase of pure water, from which it often
emerges a perfect blank. Sometimes a
few lines, at others a few words, sometimes only a punctuation mark, survive
the test. This troubles the old man. At
last he rises and leaves the room. Fable
springs to his vacant seat, and scribbles
as if in play till his return, when History
reproves her for wasting the paper, and
passes the sheet to Sophia, when, lo! it
comes out from her vase unchanged.
Fable has borne the test of Truth. History is enraged at this, and succeeds in
driving both Sophia and Fable from their
home, unfairly. Sophia is driven away,
but the child escapes by a back door, and,
becoming bewildered in the central cav-
erns of the Earth, falls into the power of
the Fates.

These respectable old ladies find the
little Fable very troublesome, and, after
some scolding, send her away to spin,

when, lo! from the recesses of the cavern all sorts of wonders and strange shapes are spun out. The Fates are frightened, and they seek History to learn in what manner they may best rid themselves of the intruder. However much they may dislike her, she is under their protection, and History can do no more than advise them to send her out to catch Tarantulas! Fable departs and meets Eros, who gives her a lyre, upon which she plays, and the venomous insects swarm about her. The Fates behold her return unharmed! They had hoped she would be stung to death, and in despair Ate throws her scissors at the child, who gracefully avoids them. Hereupon the Tarantulas sting the Fates in the feet, at which they begin to dance. As their clothes are thick and heavy, this is rather inconvenient exercise, and when Fable laughs at their distress they

send her away to spin them some thin
dresses. Fable is tired of wandering.
She plays upon her lyre to the Tarantulas, bidding them spin, and she will give
them three large flies. When the dresses
are done, she carries them immediately
to the Fates, who begin again to dance.
The ends of the threads are still in the
bodies of the Tarantulas, who do not like
to be jerked about. "Behold the flies
which I promised you," said Fable.

Thereupon the Tarantulas fall upon
the dancing Fates, and a new dynasty
commences, in which Eros reigns, with
Fable for prime minister.

MARGARET said that in the story she
had told she had set us the example
of wandering from the subject, but she
hoped to some purpose. She hoped no
one would have need to call upon little
Fable's body-guard of Tarantulas.

The subject of the evening was Apollo

in contrast with Ceres, or Genius opposed
to Productive Energy. The history of
Apollo stood for the history of thought,
its progressive development and its un-
happiness. All the loves of Apollo are
miserable. He never labors for himself.
He uses the instruments which others
have shaped. He is so delighted with
the lyre, which Mercury, that is Sagacity, has made, that he gives him the
divining-rod, and would give him more,
but he cannot. The earnest simplicity
with which Apollo begs Mercury to swear
by the sacred Styx not to steal his
quiver or his darts is beautiful! The
common understanding, mere human
sagacity, may indeed lay hands on the
weapons of the Inspired One, but it cannot possess them. The ray, the dart,
the quiver, of Apollo all stand for the
instantaneous power of thought.

Delphi did not originally belong to

Apollo. With the aid of Bacchus, he wrested it from Terra, Neptune, and Themis; hence the name "Delphi," or "The brothers." This is only another instance of his independence. All things are made to his hand. The great contrast between Ceres and Apollo lies in the success of each. Ceres is always full, always prepared to meet the call of humanity. Apollo is always unsatisfied. He transmutes whatever he touches, as he did one of his many loves, changed to a bay-tree. His changes are always beautiful.

JAMES F. CLARKE asked how Margaret would explain the fraternal relation between Bacchus and Apollo.

"Don't you remember?" she retorted. "I don't like to repeat it, it is so smart and ingenious!" Apollo and Bacchus seemed to her the question and the response. Bacchus was what the earth yielded to the touch of Genius. The grape was genial. It typified the excess of the earth's fruitfulness. Bacchus avenges the wrongs of Apollo, who is said never to have seen a shadow! He never perceives an obstacle, but instantly destroys an alien nature. Whatever opposed Apollo met with terrible retribution, — if not from himself, then from others. Genius cannot endure the presence of anything that mocks at it.

CHARLES WHEELER said something about the flaying of Marsyas.

MARGARET said that this once seemed to her the most shocking of cruelties, but she had lately seen a picture which reconciled her to the deed! After looking at the self-complacent face of Marsyas, she did not wonder that Apollo destroyed him. She longed to *see him do it!* Apollo was never indignant at any sublime treachery. He forgave Mercury his theft because it was god-like, because he did it so well.

MRS. RUSSELL said ironically that the destruction of the children of Niobe must have been a gratifying sight.

MARGARET laughed, and said, " That is like being reminded of the ' poor mariner,' when I say that I like to hear the wind blow." The indignation of Apollo seemed to her one of his noblest attributes. His perfect purity separated him from all the Gods. Ceres seemed to be included in the idea of many other Gods, as in Pan, Bacchus, Juno, and Isis; but Apollo, the divine Genius, stands alone. There is none like him.

HENRY HEDGE asked whether holiness appertained to Apollo.

MARGARET thought not. Holiness supposed a voluntary consecration of one's self, but there was no need of this

in Apollo. He was pure thought, consecrated, but not consciously.

HENRY HEDGE said he had asked, because, considering Jesus to have, as he
certainly had, a mythological character,
he thought there was a resemblance
between him and Apollo. His own
words justified the idea, — " I am the
light of the world," and so on.

MRS. RUSSELL asked suddenly why
Apollo's lyre had seven strings.

MARGARET said seven was a consecrated number.

MRS. RUSSELL asked if it did not have
to do with the seven planets?

GEORGE RIPLEY said there were not
so many in that day.

MARGARET liked the reason, and wished
she had thought of it herself!

Some one asked about the connection
between Diana and Apollo.

MARGARET said that Genius needed a sister to console him.

EMERSON asked what bearing the inscription over the Delphic temple had upon the story of Apollo, — the Divine pun EI, which means equally " Thou art" and " If," — as grand a pun as that of him who, dying, said he was going to see the great " Perhaps " ! — " le grand peut-être."

Better translated, I thought, as the great " May-be."

GEORGE RIPLEY asked if it were not generally accepted positively as " Thou art " ?

" Probably," MR. EMERSON said.

HENRY HEDGE found another type of the Apollo in the Egyptian Horus.

MRS. RUSSELL asked if the two Greek vowels had not once stood for Isis and Osiris. If so, they would have a natural connection with the oracle.

I remembered the inscription on the statue of Isis, " I am all that has been and that shall be, and none among mortals has taken off my veil." The " I am " of the Jews, and the " Thou art " of the Delphic temple are epigrammatic, but the same.

EMERSON, replying somewhat curtly to Mrs. Russell, said there were various explanations.

The story of Phaeton came next.

HENRY HEDGE asked how Presumption should be the child of Genius.

" Genius must be self-confident," Margaret said, " and that might predominate."

I asked if real Genius did not know its own resources and husband them.

MARGARET thought Genius often attempted more than it could do.

I said a man might have genius and presume, but that if *he were a genius* I should expect him to be modest. Still, as it must have a crowd of imitators, it might become the father of presumption. The substance creates the shadow.

WILLIAM STORY said no product could be as great as the producing power; but that did not seem to me to touch the point, for the question was not whether Apollo could not give birth to something less than himself, but whether the possession of power could create an unfounded claim to it.

The story of Latona followed.

HENRY HEDGE said that the word meant concealment.

MARGARET thought this very expressive, and said that the isolation which Goethe and other geniuses had been craving since the world began Apollo had no need to seek. His mother was concealment. The oracle was then discussed, — how it was possible to consult it many times and receive each time a different answer, — how it could be bribed, as by Alexander, or would give two answers in one; but nothing very new was said.

I remembered the double answer of the Pythoness to Crœsus when he meditated crossing the Halys. "Thou shalt destroy a great empire," she said. He thought it was the enemy's: fate decided it should be his own.

SOPHIA RIPLEY thought the oracle belonged to Wisdom rather than Genius.

MARGARET said Minerva dwelt in men's houses. It was necessary a voice from Heaven should speak.

Some one wondered that Jupiter had not possessed himself of the oracle, which led MARGARET back to her exponents, and she confessed that she was not quite satisfied with her own definition of Jupiter as Will.

EMERSON suggested that experience

was a prominent feature in the Jupiter, and named him Character.

Character is educated Will, said MARGARET, hesitating, and paused, for the term did not suit her.

Juno was then spoken of as passive Will, and her traits were dwelt upon. It is amusing to see how weak the Queen of Olympus can be in opposition to its King. The peacock was probably made sacred to her on account of the beauty of its plumage, while the eagle was consecrated to Jupiter on account of its strength.

I said that the peacock, strutting with conceit, glancing at its ill-shaped feet and vexed enough to bawl in consequence, easily suggested the scolding Juno.

Some one asked a question about Æsculapius. MARGARET said he was genius made practical.

HENRY HEDGE thought that Apollo by his own connection with the healing art became the symbol of physical life and beauty.

WILLIAM STORY thought no statue could bear comparison with the Apollo Belvedere.

MARGARET preferred the Antinous.

JAMES CLARKE asked why Art should present a so much more inspiring view of Greek Mythology than Poetry.

MARGARET said that all her ideas of it were deduced from Art. She did not profess to know much of the Greek authors, and depended chiefly upon Homer, but wished that some of the gentlemen who ought to know more would speak.

WILLIAM STORY thought it was because the poets wrote for popular applause, for recitation and its immediate effect. Sculptors labored more purely for their Art.

I thought too that the dramatists often had a political aim, and manœuvred Olympus to suit it!

JAMES CLARKE said that if in our time every public speaker must bend to his audience to a degree, it was still more necessary in Greece.

We were told to consider Minerva for the next conversation, and to write down our thoughts about her. For my part I don't like using Latin names for Greek deities. It greatly confuses my ideas. Jupiter and Zeus seem very different to me.

In regard to the story that Apollo never saw a shadow, CAROLINE STURGIS asked how Apollo could destroy an alien nature if he never met it.

There was quite an unsatisfactory talk about this, which would have ended had anybody remembered how the sun solves the enigma every day. The sun never sees the shadow it destroys. When its rays fall, light is. It annihilates the alien by merely being. So Truth annihilates Falsehood, yet cannot meet it. The two are never in one presence.

CAROLINE WELLS HEALEY.

March 20, 1841.

IV.

March 26, 1841.

MARGARET opened our talk by saying that the subject of Wisdom presented more conversable points than that of Genius. We could all think and talk about Wisdom, and any man who had ever scratched his finger was to a degree wise.

Minerva was the child of Counsel and Intelligent Will. She had no infancy, but sprang full-armed into being. Ready, agile, she was in herself the history of thought. She did not need that her life should be one of incident. Her attendant emblems are expressive : the Sphinx, the owl, the serpent, the cock, and the javelin suggest her whole story.

WILLIAM WHITE asked why Genius was masculine and Wisdom feminine.

MARGARET thought no one could find any difficulty in the fact that Genius was masculine. It presented itself to the mind in the full glow of power. The very outlines of the feminine form were yielding, and we could not associate them with a prominent, self-conscious state of the faculties. Wisdom was like woman, always ready for the fight if necessary, yet never going to it; taking reality as a basis, and classifying and arranging upon it all that Genius creates, — seeing the relations and proper values of things.

GEORGE RILPEY objected to this definition. He might have imbibed a Hebrew idea, but the office of Wisdom was surely something more than this, — a purely mechanical and orderly tact.

MARGARET said she had not meant to

give *our* view of it, only the Greek idea as manifest in the story of Minerva. To William White she said, smiling, that she supposed he had not wondered so much that Genius should be masculine as that Wisdom should be feminine! But the Greeks were wise, and she revered their keen perception.

ELISABETH HOAR said it seemed to her that Wisdom provided *means.* A hero might be inspired by Genius, but Wisdom provided his armor, taught him to distinguish the goal, and to perceive clearly the relation to it of any onward step.

MARGARET agreed to this, and

WILLIAM STORY said that Genius was indebted to Wisdom for *means of communication.* Genius thinks words impertinent, but Wisdom apprehends its intuitions, and gives them shape.

MARGARET said further, that Wisdom

must adopt instinctively the finest medium.

It seemed to me that Wisdom not only gave power of communication, but power of attainment. Walter Scott was a good instance of the union of intuitive perception and human sagacity, but all these words about it cleared up nothing.

MARGARET then proposed that we should take up the attributes of Minerva, and so get at the facts.

MR. RIPLEY did not think it noble enough when she based Wisdom upon realities.

WILLIAM STORY said Wisdom must have something to work upon. He thought Wisdom compared the intuitions of Genius with realities.

CHARLES WHEELER thought the word *actual* would help them out of their difficulty.

I wanted to quote Emerson to the

effect that the Ideal is more Real than the Actual.

MARGARET agreed with Mr. Wheeler, and said that by reality she understood anything incarnated, — whatever was tangible. She then went on to speak of the Sphinx. What was it?

ELISABETH HOAR seemed surprised at the question. Was it not one thing to everybody?

MARGARET called for her idea, but she would not give it.

MARGARET said that to herself it represented the development of a thought, founding itself upon the animal, until it grew upward into calm, placid power. She revered these good ancients, who did not throw away any of the gifts of God; who were neither materialists nor immaterialists, but who made matter always subservient to the highest ends of the Spirit.

6

William White asked if the festivals of the Gods, the highest source of their influence over the people, did not show how little they had penetrated to the spirit of things?

Margaret thought ambrosia and nectar were proper emblems of Divine Joy. They were not to be taken literally.

"But," persisted White, "the great body of the people thought them so."

William Story said, with happy grace, that the great *body* of the people might be excused for such a thought.

Margaret enjoyed the pun, and said that the great Greek body was sensuous and ate, but that the Greek soul knew better than to suspect the Gods of opening their mouths.

E. P. P. waked up at this moment, and asked what Margaret would say to Berkeley's theory.

MARGARET said she did not know what it was!

E. P. P. said, the evolution of all things from the soul, the non-existence of matter.

JAMES F. CLARKE thought it very difficult to decide how far spirit and matter were one. A man's identity was not in the particles which came and went every seven years, but in the spirit. Yet these particles constituted the wall of separation between himself and others. His identity was in his spirit.

GEORGE RIPLEY begged leave to disagree. He thought we knew as much about matter as about spirit, and that Berkeley's theory was as good as any.

MARGARET said that if God created matter, of course it was evolved from spirit; that matter could not be antagonistic to that from which it was evolved.

To express a complete idea, we had only to say, " Jehovah, I am."

" Or," CHARLES WHEELER added, " to be silent."

" Yes," said MARGARET, " and in that lies the merit of Mythology. Every faculty was, according to that, an incomplete statement. Therefore Mr. Ripley did wrong to confound Minerva with the Logos."

E. P. P. did not see that Berkeley's statement was answered.

WILLIAM STORY came in with another pun. " If Berkeley thought so, it was *no matter !* "

Some stupid person spoiled the wit by trying to explain it, and the question remained to us just as much matter as ever.

They talked about the Sphinx again, yet said little. It holds more meaning in its passive womb than talk will ever

play the midwife to. It was the child of
the Destructive Element and Feeling,
— Typhon and Echidna, — the human
heart experienced in misfortune touched
by death. Thought rooted in the actual
and developed by tenderness was rooted
in this figure.

"Everybody knows that Wisdom
stings," said MARGARET, and so we went
on to the serpent.

Somebody spoke of the Greek Tartarus.

IDA RUSSELL thought its torment was
not acute, but consisted of the depriva-
tion of comforts.

The wandering idleness of it would be
intolerable to an active Greek, ELISA-
BETH HOAR thought, but more endurable than any device of a priesthood. As
for our serpent, no one seemed to know
much about it.

MARGARET said that we owed it so

much, that *she* felt in duty bound to know something of it.

JAMES F. CLARKE said that the Christian serpent was quite another thing.

Everybody laughed at the idea of a *Christian* serpent.

WILLIAM WHITE professed great admiration for the reptile. We should have had no Christianity but for its beguiling.

MARGARET agreed! — and said she supposed everybody felt that.

MRS. RUSSELL thought the casting of the skin very expressive.

JAMES F. CLARKE gave Coleridge's exposition, to the effect that the serpent was the common understanding! It would touch and handle all things, and even sought to be as the Gods, knowing good from evil. Its undulating motion — its belly now on the ground, now off

— expressed both the aspiration and the subserviency of the creature.

MARGARET asked if serpents ever swallowed their own tails?

CHARLES WHEELER said that must be an arbitrary form.

MARGARET replied, that she had been struck by the difference between the Mexican and the Greek serpent. The Mexican was folded back upon itself.

Not always, I said. Its tail is sometimes in its mouth, and the variations seem to be occasioned by the architectural necessity.

JAMES F. CLARKE spoke of a Virginia snake that moves in a circle, and asked if when Mr. Emerson talked about " coming full circle " he was not thinking of that?

MARGARET laughed, and declared that serpent must be of Yankee invention. Æsculapius bore two on his staff, Mercury two on his divining-rod, and the cock was also sacred to Æsculapius.

I asked if this did not indicate a certain subjection of these Gods to Wisdom?

Some questions written on paper were here read. One asked why Minerva was born of the stroke of Vulcan, and why she was the patroness of weavers, and what that had to do with the story of Arachne.

MARGARET replied with ill temper to the first, that it was because Vulcan held the hammer, — to the second, that she did not know.

But was there really so little meaning in the fact that Mechanic Art so ministered to Intelligent Will that she could afford to miss the point?

She said we could see that Minerva was told to marry Vulcan, but declined; would have nothing to do with the sooty cripple.

SOPHIA RIPLEY said, aptly enough, that Minerva had been changing her mind ever since!

IDA RUSSELL thought that when Mechanic Art was married to Beauty, it might charm even Wisdom.

GEORGE RIPLEY said she might well have despised the brute force, but as it grew into something more noble, have learned to love it. Dr. Dana[1] was the servant of the Lowell corporation. In these days no corporation could exist without its man of science. His salary was a mere pittance, and when he made a discovery with which all Europe rang,

---

[1] Dr. Dana, a celebrated chemist, received a salary from the Merrimac Manufacturing Co. as consulting chemist. Through his experiments and practical skill, a radical change was made in the methods of dyeing and printing calicoes. This was in connection with the use of madder, and the Company claimed his discovery and allowed him no extra recompense. It will be perceived that Mr. Ripley got his supposed facts from the newspapers.

he asked for a part of the profits. " We will consider," said the soulless corporation, and they decided that they had a legitimate right to all that could be made out of their servant!

" Thus," I said, " Wisdom sows for the Mechanic Art to reap ? "

" Exactly so," was the reply; " and this contains the essence of the Yankee philosophy."

The life of Wisdom was one long struggle for something beyond a merely serviceable knowledge. Bending alike to art and artisan, she still refused to love the latter till he had wooed Beauty to their common service. But Wisdom has of late married Vulcan. He no longer limps, and has washed his face in the springs of love and thought, and sits in holiday robes beside his bride.

Somebody said that the story of

Arachne was an instance of the Goddess's vindictiveness.

MARGARET hoped that the vindictiveness was a popular interpolation. If so, the story of Marsyas shows that she was malicious. She brought his misfortunes upon him. If her own voice was discordant, there was no reason why his voice should please!

"Divinities have a right to be indignant," said somebody. Did Margaret blush?

In speaking of the artistic representations of Minerva, MARGARET said some beautiful things. Minerva was as tall and large as she could be, without being masculine. Her face was thoughtful and serene, without being sweet. Her eye was so full and clear that it had no need to be deep.

The talk was closed by Margaret's

reading the Essay that E. P. P. had sent in, and the criticisms upon it.

E. P. P. began by speaking of the *conservatism* which disinclined Jupiter to the birth of Minerva.

"Yes," MARGARET said, "the good was always opposed to the better."

E. P. P. then spoke of the Parthenon, upon which, according to the Homeric Hymn, the story of Minerva's birth was sculptured.

MARGARET said it had been difficult to believe that the Greeks would put so ugly a thing upon their temple, but the ruins showed a Vulcan with his hammer in his hand, and the form of the Goddess hovering over the cloven skull.

Why, asked E. P. P., did Ulysses represent Wisdom in the Odyssey?

MARGARET thought he represented the history of a thought in life, when he tired us all out with his long story, and so pushed us to decision.

E. P. P. alluded to the different conceptions of Minerva in the Iliad and the Odyssey, and this led to the question of priority of composition.

MARGARET thought the Odyssey was written when Homer was young and romantic; but E. P. P. and myself stood out stoutly for the precedence of the Iliad. I said, without the least bit of real knowledge, that I should not wonder if there were two centuries between the poems, they seemed to indicate such entirely different states of society; but certainly the Odyssey was latest.

CHARLES WHEELER said that the best scholars seemed all of one mind. The Iliad was written first by Homer, — the Odyssey long after by another hand.

E. P. P. said that there was a gem which represented Minerva as married to a mortal, but she could tell nothing more about it.

Jones Very said that when Wisdom falls into decay we call it Genius!

Does that mean that prophetic power fallen back from the moral nature to the intellect is dwarfed accordingly?

CAROLINE W. HEALEY.

March 27, 1841.

V.

THE story of Venus and Cupid and Psyche was discussed.

MARGARET said that of Venus she had less to say than of either of the preceding Deities! She was not the expression of a thought, but of a fact. She was the Greek idea of a lovely woman, — the best physical development of woman. When we have said, "It is," we have said all. The birth of Beauty was the only ideal thing about her. She sprang from the wave, from the flux and reflux of things, from the undulating line. On this Venus, transitoriness had set its seal. As we look at her, we feel that she must change. Her loveliness is too fair to last. Her beauty would pass next moment. She could not live a year, we think, without losing something of her full grace. It was peculiarly Greek to create a beautiful symbol, and to pause in the symbol. The Greeks were very apt to do this. They did it effectually in the Goddess of Love. She was sportive in all her amours. They had no idea of an Everlasting Love. They enjoyed themselves too much to abstract themselves. Venus seemed to Margaret a merely human creature. She was not the type of Universal Beauty: the Greek eye was closed to that. Still, their own embodiment did not satisfy their own need. They filled out their ideal with Venus Urania, Hebe, and all the attendant Hours and Graces, yet were not satisfied. Then came the fable of Psyche and her three Cupids. Venus was only a pretty girl! Her cestus, her doves, her pets, her jealousies, all betray it. The Venus Urania was more. *She* was the child of Celestial Light. Hebe was born of immortal bloom. To fill out the gaps in their conception, Eros, or Love in Sadness, Cupid a frolicsome boy, and the more noble, more creative Love which brooded over Chaos were evolved from their consciousness. Psyche, who did not appear until the age of Augustus, who was too modern to be mythological, yet glowing with mythic beauty, was only another evidence of their imperfect idea. Her story expresses more than that of Venus. It tells not only the story of human love, but represents the pilgrimage of a soul. The jealousy of Venus was that which the good must always feel toward the better which is to supersede it, and as soon as Psyche looked upon her sleeping lover she became immortal. The soul in the fulness of Love became conscious of Destiny.

7

JAMES CLARKE asked what was the difference between the girl-mother — the Madonna — and the Greek Venus.

MARGARET replied, with more patience than I was capable of, that the Madonna represented more than passing womanly beauty. She was prophetic, and lived again in her child.

Then, persisted JAMES F., why was Vulcan the *husband* of Beauty, to which Margaret gave no satisfactory answer. He then gave his own thought, to which I can do no justice, although it was what I tried in vain to say at the last conversation. It amounted to this, — that in seeking for beauty we lose it, but in aiming at utility through hard labor we find perfect proportion — and consequently perfect beauty. He said that he and his sister Sarah had often spoken to each other about this, and he felt that the time would come when essays would be written about our ships, as we now write essays about the Pyramids and the Greek Art. Posterity might find the proof of our search after beauty in the graceful prow and swelling hold and tall, tapering mast or shrouds of shredded jet; in the bellying canvas and the patron saint which watches the wake from the stern. But we know that the ship, the most beautiful object in our modern world, was the product of labor, gradually evoked, according to the law of fitness, compass, and general proportion. To bring its form into a natural relation to wind and wave, was to find perfect harmony and beauty. At first the prow was too sharp, and the water had rushed over it; the hold was too shallow, and she sat ungracefully where she now rides as mistress.

EMERSON quoted some German author to the same effect.

MR. CLARKE said there was something in one of R. W. E.'s own Essays which expressed the same thing.

EMERSON laughed and said, " Very important authority," and would have changed the subject, when —

WILLIAM WHITE said that it did not tally well with James Clarke's theory that the ugly steamer had succeeded the beautiful clipper.

MR. CLARKE said the theory failed only because there was no noble end in view. The steamer was not intended to be in harmony with Nature.

EMERSON asked if the Greeks had no symbol for natural beauty. Several were suggested that he would not accept, but he finally took Diana on Charles Wheeler's suggestion.

WHEELER then spoke of the birth of Venus. He said many writers thought the story as late as that of Psyche, and the line of Hesiod relating to it an interpolation.

MARGARET thought she should have suspected this if she had never heard it. The thought it expressed was too comprehensive to be in keeping with the remainder of her story.

CHARLES WHEELER would not accept the criticism, but went on to talk about the marriage of Venus with Mars, which had amazed Olympus.

MARGARET said the Olympian Deities were like modern men, who talk to women forever about their softness and delicacy, until women imagine that the only good thing in man is a strong arm. The girl elopes with a red coat, and the indignant lords of creation wonder why she did not appreciate their modest merit and unobtrusive virtues. Poor Beauty *weeps out* the crimson stain upon her escutcheon in a long age of suffering.

A laugh followed this bright sally, and then somebody said that Venus once married Mercury.

MARGARET declared that must be an interpolation, for there were no points of sympathy between the Goddess of beauty and the God of craft.

JAMES CLARKE did not know about that; he thought that the finish and completeness of the late robbery of Davis, Palmer, & Co. constituted a *kind of beauty!*

MARGARET said that affair was altogether grand; she had never heard of anything so Greek as Williamson's exclaiming, "Gentlemen! you will not deprive me of the implements of my trade?" She could not help respecting his impudence! The Greeks ought to be respected for developing every human faculty into deity. She thought lying, stealing, and so forth only excesses of a good faculty; and so did the Greeks, for in their mistaken way they had deified Mercury. The Spartans taught their children to steal, and the Greeks universally acknowledged that to cheat was honorable if it could be concealed.

I remembered the passage in the "Republic" where Polemarchus confesses that he had learned from Homer to admire Autolycus, grandsire of Ulysses, distinguished above all men for his thefts and oaths! Thrasymachus said that the unjust were both prudent and good, if they were able to commit injustice to *perfection!* Is the immortality of Autolycus the destiny of Williamson?

WHEELER said there certainly was a well authenticated marriage between Venus and Mercury.

I could not help thinking it might be an astral connection that was indicated. On that remarkable day of his birth,

Mercury was not content with stealing the divining-rod from Apollo; he took also the cestus from Venus, the voice from Neptune, the sword from Mars, the will from Zeus, and his tools from Vulcan! Sagacity compassed all the deeps of divinity to reach its end.

IDA RUSSELL asked if Venus and Astarte were not the same.

MARGARET said Astarte belonged to the stars.

Did not Venus, I wonder? But of course they are creations far asunder as the poles.

CHARLES WHEELER thought Astarte and Venus Urania were the same.

IDA said that could not be. The first statues of Astarte were rough blocks of wood, with veiled heads.

So, I said, were all first statues of Deities; so that was no argument.

When JAMES CLARKE asked Margaret

to compare Venus with the Madonna, a curious talk arose between Alcott, Margaret, Charles Wheeler, and Emerson.

ALCOTT wanted to know why Christ was not as much an impersonation of a human faculty as either of the Greek Deities!

MARGARET said Jesus was not a thought. He was born on the earth, and lived out a thought. He was no abstraction to her, but a brother.

ALCOTT wanted to know whether a purer mythology, suited to the wants of coming time, might not arise from the mixed mythology of Persians, Greeks, and Christians!

A very confusing and tiresome talk arose thereupon, which Charles Wheeler smiled at, but did not join in, and which profited nobody.

CAROLINE WELLS HEALEY.

April 3, 1841.

VI.

CUPID AND PSYCHE.

April 9, 1841.

MARGARET thought it would be very impertinent to begin by telling what everybody knew, — the old story of Cupid and Psyche.

E. P. P. declared that Margaret never told it twice alike, and at last she yielded and said : —

The beautiful young princess Psyche was envied by Venus, who sent Eros to destroy her; but the God, finding Psyche wholly lovely, wedded her. They lived happily until Psyche began to doubt. Eros had told her that she must not seek to know him; but curiosity prevailed over faith, and in looking at him as he slept she wounded and waked him. He left her in dismay; and as a punishment the three trials which are the lot of mortals were awarded to her. She must sort grain, she must bring three drops from the river Styx, and must get the box of beauty from Proserpine. The birds helped her with the grain; but when she reached the banks of the Styx and stooped to fulfil the second task, she found the water too dark, too cold, and the eagle came to her aid. At the prospect of the third trial her soul sank; she refused to undertake it; but, winning from one of the Gods the secret of self-dependence, she set off for Tartarus, gave the usual sop to Cerberus, and returned with her prize. But she was "possessed" with the idea that the treasures the box contained might restore to her her husband's love, and she opened the box as she came. The noxious vapors which issued from it deprived her of consciousness, and she fell. Eros, who had flown to seek her as soon as his wound was healed, brought her the gift of Immortality which he had begged of Jupiter.

ELISABETH HOAR asked what had become of Psyche's sisters, whose inter- ference was a striking point in the story.

MARGARET said she knew nothing of them, and wished Miss Hoar would tell us. Her own knowledge of the story was gained entirely from Raphael's original studies, and his frescos on the walls of a Roman palace.

ELISABETH HOAR recapitulated. The parents of Psyche were ordered by the angry Venus to expose her upon a high mountain, when Zephyr carried her to the embraces of Love, who dwelt in the depths of a quiet valley hard by. Her sisters came to bewail her death, and

Psyche begged Love to let Zephyr bring them to rejoice in her happiness. For some time he refused, telling her that it was not for her good, and that she could be happy without them. This our foolish Psyche would not believe, and at last they were permitted to come, only she must not tell them the little she knew about her husband.

The first time Psyche had sent them away loaded with gifts. They had questioned her about her husband, and Psyche replied that he was only a lovely child. The year went round, and again the lovely bride longed for her sisters' presence. Again the God entreated her to be patient, assuring her that if they came it would only be to make her miserable. Psyche could not be quieted. Again they came, again they questioned. She forgot the story she had previously told, and replied that he was an old man, bent with years, but very kind to her. Then the envious women saw that Psyche was herself ignorant of his true nature. They told her that he was a dragon, and meant to devour her; that they had themselves seen him as he passed through the fields. They begged her to take a knife and lamp and kill him as he slept. The frightened Psyche consented.

The God was sleeping in radiant beauty at her side, and as she gazed upon him she drew an arrow from his quiver and carelessly scratched her finger. Impassioned by the wound, she bent over him, and a drop of scalding oil fell from her lamp. Angry and confused, the God awoke, and, irritated by the pain, flew away. Psyche clung to him; but she could not support herself, and he was too angry to hold her. She fell to the ground, and he, perched upon a neighboring tree, reproached her.

MARGARET did not know this, but said she remembered that Psyche tried to drown herself.

ELISABETH said that was later. She despaired, and threw herself into the river; but the river pitied her, and bore her to the shore. Venus, growing tired of her guest, sent Mercury to advertise her. Psyche yielded to the terms of the Goddess, rendered herself up, and was busy sorting the gifts in the temple of Beauty when Custom was sent to berate her.

This, I suppose, is a condensation of the lovely allegory of Apuleius in the second century of our era, but it seems to me Elisabeth made some additions.

MARGARET said that everybody had to contend with the meddlesome sisters. They were at the bottom of every fairy story, from that of Psyche to Beauty and the Beast.

ELISABETH HOAR said it was always with the young soul as it was with Psyche. It could give no account of the love which made it so happy.

So, I said, every human heart shrivels under a curious touch. Love is angry that we wound him, and if he ever does return it is with Immortality in his hand. When custom berates, God accepts.

JAMES CLARKE asked if there was not a celebrated statue of Cupid and Psyche.

MARGARET had only heard of Canova's, but James said he was sure there was one older.

WILLIAM STORY asked if it were older than Apuleius, but James did not know.

IDA RUSSELL said it was wrong for Psyche to look.

Yes, MARGARET said, but her temptations were strong; and if they had not come through her sisters, they must have come through her own soul. Everything was produced by antagonism. This morning she had taken up Kreitzer, meaning to open the Greek volume, but took up the Indian. In that Mythology which William Story called deep and all-embracing there were the antagonist principles of Vishnu, or unclouded innocence, and Brahm, who could only become pure by wading through all wickedness. There seemed to be a need of sin, to work out salvation for human beings.

EMERSON said faith should work out that salvation. It was man's privilege to resist the evil, to strive triumphantly; to recognise it — never! Good was always present to the soul, — was all the true soul took note of. It was a duty not to look!

MARGARET thought it the climax of sin to despair. She believed evil to be a good in the grand scheme of things. She would not recognize it as a blunder.

She must consider its scope a noble one. In one word, she would not accept the world — for she felt within herself the power to reject it — did she not believe evil working in it for good! Man had gained more than he lost by his fall. The ninety-nine sheep in the parable were of less value than the " lost found," over which there was joy in heaven.

E. P. P. spoke of the Tree of Life, — which would have made immortal those who ate of the Tree of Knowledge.

CAROLINE STURGIS said that this probation was what she could not comprehend. We began at the circumference, and if we fulfilled our destiny must end by being near the centre. How much better to have begun there! Why could not God have made it so?

WILLIAM STORY began to say that God must seek the best good of all his creatures ; but Caroline interrupted him by saying that there was certainly more good at the centre than at the circumference.

WILLIAM WHITE thought all this good, better, and best very puzzling.

MARGARET asked Caroline if she could not see probation to be a good, as she had herself defined it?

Are we better then, than God? asked CAROLINE.

Not better, replied MARGARET, for we cannot compare dissimilar things.

WILLIAM WHITE asked if any one could be more than good, more than pure.

WILLIAM STORY said perfection had its degrees!

WHITE said, How can you progress after you have reached your goal?

As if any live man ever *did* reach his goal! said I.

Is there any progress for God? retorted he.

Not any, for that is a contradiction in terms, I said; but surely you conceive of it for souls in heaven?

MARGARET said something about the Gospel injunction to be perfect even as our Father in Heaven is perfect. Does not "even as" mean "after the pattern of"? Does it involve the *nature*, as well as the *degree?*

EMERSON interrupted quickly, "We are not finite."

Everybody smiled; but the best answer to this is found in the fact, that we never conceive of ourselves as infinite and at rest, — only as reaching after the Infinite in our motion.

WHITE said to Caroline Sturgis, "If evil brings knowledge of good, is it not a gain?"

WILLIAM STORY talked nobly, something to this effect: That good and evil were related terms. If both did not exist, neither could, antagonism being the spring of most things in the universe.

MARGARET went back to Cupid, and said that in Raphael's original studies Cupid was always a boy, — in his frescos, a youth, almost a man. She spoke of the difference of expression which he gave to his Venus and his Psyche, especially in the eye. That of Psyche was deep and thoughtful. The distinction extended to their attendant Cupids, and was most marked in the Psyche when she takes the cup of Immortality from her husband.

MARGARET wanted to pass on to Diana, but there were too many clergymen in the company. Everybody was interested in somebody nearer at hand, and views of the unchanging Providence were next presented.

MARGARET said God was the background against which all creation was thrown.

WILLIAM STORY asked if she did not think He was greater than his creatures?

"Always beyond," was MARGARET'S reply.

Creation, STORY said, was rather the exponent of a *Love* which *must bless*, than of an activity which must act. It was a Paternal power that *ruled*, not an autocratic power which *fathered* us.

MARGARET said that the story of Cupid and Psyche was the story of redemption. It contained the seeds of the doctrine of election, — saving by grace, and so on!

A good many queer things were said on various points touched by this.

EMERSON said, that to imagine it possible to fall was to *begin* to fall.

E. P. P. got into a little maze trying to introduce Margaret and R. W. E.

to each other, — a consummation which, however devoutly to be wished, will never happen!

JAMES CLARKE told her that she was just where Paul was when he said, "What then? Shall I sin, that Grace may the more abound?"

EMERSON said the woodlands could tell us most about Diana, about whom we contrived to say very little. The omission of orgies in her worship was dwelt upon. Her pure and sacred character with the Athenians was compared to that of the Diana of Ephesus, whose orgies were not unusual, and who was considered as a bountiful mother rather than as a virgin huntress.

IDA RUSSELL said that *her* Mythology accused Diana of being the mother of fifty sons and fifty daughters!

MARGARET laughed, and said that certainly was Diana of Ephesus!

The maddening influence of moonlight was commented upon, as if it were a fable ; but WILLIAM STORY said it was a fact. In tropical regions very sad consequences resulted from long gazing on the moonlight or sleeping in it. In one town he had known sixteen persons bewildered in this way.

WILLIAM WHITE said that in a late book of Nichols it was contended that the moon had some light of her own, because she shows a brazen color even under eclipse, when the dark side of the earth is toward her. But why may she not gather stellar light from the whole universe, as the earth seems to ?

SALLIE GARDINER said something to William Story in a low voice. He laughed, and said he had been thinking of the consequences of his theory.

MARGARET asked what he was talking about.

STORY said it was an application of eclipses to his theory that love was the motive to creation. If the sun is beneficent truth shorn of its beams, it would be like the moon, no better than brass!

CAROLINE STURGIS asked why the Mahomedans bore the crescent.

WILLIAM WHITE said because of some change in the moon which occurred at the time of the Hegira.

WILLIAM STORY said that the worshippers at Mecca carried the crescent before Mahomet's time. There is a crescent on the black stone.

Both stories may be true. There is certainly a crescent on the old Byzantine coin, or besant.

IDA RUSSELL said something about Diana being wedded.

This reminded E. P. P. of Minerva's marriage, discussed last week. She said that Charles Wheeler had seen the gem of which she then spoke, and that Neptune was the favored suitor.

WILLIAM STORY said the Greeks could not wed Neptune to Diana, for the tides were too low in the Mediterranean!

C. W. HEALEY.

April 10, 1841.

VII.

PLUTO AND TARTARUS.

April 15, 1841.

MARGARET said very little about Pluto. On the first evening she had called him the depth of things, and JAMES CLARKE now had a good deal to say upon the three ideas which she thought pervaded the Greek mythology, — the source, the depth, and the extent or flow of thought. He said that this distinction had struck him very forcibly when Margaret first mentioned it. We speak of widely diffused thought, of aspiring and profound thought; of sympathetic, exalted, or deep feeling, — and this seemed to exhaust language. It was through the depths of feeling and experience that we came to the profound of thought.

E. P. P. said, "There is no genius in happiness." Not a very intelligible statement.

MARGARET said, "There is nothing worth knowing that has not some penalty attached to it. We pay it the more willingly in proportion as we grow wise. Depth, altitude, diffusion, are the three births of Time. It is this which makes the German cover the operations of the miner with a mystic veil. Bostonians laugh at the Germans because they think."

WHEELER liked what Mr. Clarke said, and added that there was meaning in the Irish phrase, "*Lower me up.*"

MARGARET said that all the punishments of Tartarus expressed baffled effort, the penalty least endurable to the active Greek.

Mr. Mack thought it singular that in every nation where the belief in Tartarus had prevailed, an exact locality had always been assigned to it.

William White said that, so long as anybody could point out the locality of the garden of Eden, we had no need to smile at the locality of a Tartarus or an Elysium.

I do not think these "myths" belong to the same class.

Charles Wheeler quoted Champollion to the effect that the Styx was only a small river flowing between the Temple at Thebes and a neighboring "place of tombs." The ferryman was named Charon, and the Egyptian habit of judging the dead probably gave rise to the rest of the fable.

Margaret said, "This was very natural." She asked Mr. Wheeler the meaning of certain names.

Phlegethon, he answered, meant burning fire; Acheron, anguish.

Why did not somebody say that the lifeless current of the Styx first tempted Homer to give it to the Infernals? It is in reality a river of Epeiros.

The Styx, WHEELER said, was a cold unhealthy stream, like that which caused the death of Alexander. It flowed slowly through Acadia, but was supposed to take its rise in Hades. Lethe is a river near the Syrtus in Africa. It disappears in the sand, but rises again. Hence its name.

MR. WHEELER had some difficulty in explaining certain inconsistencies in the poets.

MR. CLARKE quoted the remark of Achilles (?) concerning Elysium, — that a day of hard labor on earth was preferable to an eternity of pleasure in Elysian fields!

MARGARET said that in Elysium, as in Tartarus, souls waited. These restless Greeks could do nothing. They were cut off from action, which was their delight. All their punishments seem to consist of frustrated effort, — the consequence of some presumption. Tantalus was ever thirsty and ever famished because he had aspired to nectar and ambrosia. Ixion, who would have scaled the heavens, was condemned to incessant revolution upon a wheel, which never paused yet never accomplished anything. The Danaides, who murdered the love which wooed them, were doomed to fill a broken vessel with water which as constantly escaped. Sisyphus, who had never labored except for a selfish end, was to roll a stone up hill, which as constantly rolled down, — fit emblem of all selfish labor. As for Tityrus, who sought to violate the secrets of Nature, the vulture fed always upon his entrails.

WHEELER said this did not represent frustrated effort.

MARGARET said, No: this was remorse; but there was an admirable instance of the former given by Goethe, of a man who wove rope from the sedges which grew upon the banks of Lethe, for an ass who continually devoured it. The moral seemed to be that the ass could just as well have eaten them unwoven. Goethe goes on to say that the Greeks only thought that the poor man had a prodigal wife, but that the moderns would look deeper and see more in the fable.

We all weave sedges for asses to eat, thought I.

MARGARET seemed to think that every heart might have an experience which would correspond to Tartarus. Every hero must visit it at least once.

I suggested Pluto, Persephone, the

Fates, the Gorgons, the Furies, and Cerberus. Pluto was equal to Neptune and Jupiter.

MARGARET continued: Hades was not given to Pluto to mark defective character, but simply as his kingdom. His wants were all supplied. The bride Olympus refused him he was permitted to steal from earth while she gathered flowers. Persephone, seed of all things, must dwell in the dark; but another legend tells us that if she had been willing to leave her veil, she might have stolen away. There was a meaning in her being forbidden to eat in the infernal regions. Fate said, "Do not touch what you don't want." Psyche was forbidden to partake of the regal banquet Persephone spread. Seeking for Immortality, this soul, like every other, must be content to eat bitter bread.

9

There was then a talk about Cerberus and the Gorgons.

Mr. Clarke said that in the New Testament the dog seemed to stand for popular prejudice. The swine stood for what *could* not, the dog for what *would* not, be convinced.

Yes, Margaret said, the wolf is a misanthropic dog. He has little dignity.

Ida Russell said Cerberus stood for the temperaments.

Well, Margaret said, that being so, she liked the Greeks for making no allowance for the lymphatic. To what, she continued, do we offer the first sop, as we pass through life? As for the Gorgons, every one, she thought, would find his own interpretation of them. To her there was no Gorgon but *apathy;* there is nothing in creation that will so soon turn a live man into stone. These Gorgons were three women, who used

one eye and one tooth between them, —
except Medusa, who was beautiful and
perfect. Her hair had provoked the
envy of Minerva, and was changed into
serpents. Margaret had a copy of a
gem, which Marion Dwight had made
for her, which showed this.

E. P. P. asked if Perseus did not en-
deavor to show Medusa her own head.

MARGARET said that might well rouse
her!

CHARLES WHEELER explained. Perseus only used a mirror given him by
Minerva to avoid looking at the Gorgon.

CAROLINE STURGIS said that the old
woman who keeps house for Helen in
the second part of "Faust" was a Gorgon
to her.

This dragged a critical analysis of
the "Faust" forward.

MARGARET said the Seeker represents
the Spirit of the Age. He never sinned

save by yielding, and yet he was emphatically *saved by grace.* It was difficult to see what Goethe meant until he got to the Tower of the Middle Ages. That made all clear.

CHARLES WHEELER said, the reader would a great deal rather that Faust went to the Devil than not!

Margaret defended Goethe's way of exhibiting character, of which Wilhelm Meister was an instance. Goethe said to himself, What should I do with a hero in such rascally society? Meister preferred the Brahmal experience.

E. P. P. asked if this moral indifference was well?

MARGARET replied, that it was just as frightful as any other Gorgon. If we are to have a purely intellectual development, it was well for a man like Goethe to represent it. To choose fairly between evil and good, the intellect must regard both with indifference.

Somebody asked how the Gorgon's head came to be on the Ægis of Minerva?

If Apathy is the Gorgon, surely Wisdom needs it!

Then we began to talk about Theseus in connection with Tartarus. Why should he sit forever on a stone?

MARGARET thought he represented reform!

MR. MACK said reform checked itself by its own fanaticism.

WHEELER, in this connection, asked after the Greek notion of accountability.

MARGARET did not think the Greeks had any.

WHEELER assured her to the contrary, and told anecdotes to prove it. He spoke of the fatal transmission of guilt in one family, generation after generation.

MARGARET said the Greeks never rejected facts.

IDA RUSSELL spoke of the last King of Athens, Codrus, supposed to have been punished for the crimes of his ancestors.

WHEELER said that when the Greeks killed some ambassadors, they felt so sure that Heaven would avenge the sin that they sent two citizens to expiate it; but Darius, to whom they were sent, refused to release the Greeks from their impending doom.

MARGARET said the moment such a supposition was started, there were plenty of facts to sustain it. Orestes is the purified victim of his family. The old Greeks had made no complete statement of their destiny or their accountability.

E. P. P. said they had made it in art.

C. W. HEALEY.

April 16, 1841.

VIII.

MERCURY AND ORPHEUS.

April 22, 1841.

MARGARET said it surprised her that young men did not seek to be Mercuries. She said that one of the ugliest young men that she knew had become so enraptured with one of Raphael's Mercuries, that he confessed to her that he was never alone without trying to assume its attitude before the glass. She said she could not help laughing at the image he suggested, an ugly figure in high-heeled boots and a strait-coat in the act of flying, commissioned with every grace from Heaven to men! but she respected the feeling, and thought every sensitive soul must share it.

EMERSON had sent Sophia Peabody several fine engravings. One of these, a Correggio, represented a woman of Parma as a Madonna. It might give any woman a similar desire.

William Story, Frank Shaw, Mr. Mack and his friends, Mrs. Ripley, Ida Russell, and Mrs. S. G. Ward were all missing to-night.

MARGARET said that she was sorry she had allowed our subject to embrace so much. The Grecian Mercury seemed to mean so little that she had not thought of the depth and difficulty connected with the Egyptian Hermes. Among the Greeks, Ceres, Persephone, and Juno represent the productive faculties, Jupiter and Apollo the divine, and Mercury simply the human understanding, the God of eloquence and of thieves.

MARIANNE JACKSON thought it strange that he should be at once the God of persuasion and the Deity of theft!

MARGARET said eloquence was a kind of thieving!

Did the Greeks so consider it? asked MARIANNE.

MARGARET said, Yes, more than any nation in the world, and taught their children so to do; and in fact such mental recognitions were what distinguished the nation from all other peoples.

The Egyptian Hermes represented the whole intellectual progress of man. If one made a discovery it was signed Hermes, and under that name transmitted to posterity. Hence the forty volumes of Hermetic theology, philosophy, and so on. Individuals were merged in the God. Hermes was always the mediator, the peacemaker, and it was in this relation that the beautiful story was told of the caduceus. Mercury has originally only the divining-rod which Apollo had given him, but, finding two serpents fighting one day, he pacified them, and had ever after the right to bear them embracing on his rod. There was another story, Margaret said, which she could not understand, — the story of his obtaining the head of the Ibis from Osiris. Hermes kept the *first* or outside gates of Heaven, a significant fact typically considered.

I am sure there is something in Heeren's researches about the Ibis story, but Caroline Sturgis said, No.

WILLIAM WHITE asked if the God gave the name to the planet?

MARGARET said, Yes; and it was given because it stood nearest the sun.

E. P. P. said Plutarch had written something about Hermes in his "Morals."

MARGARET said, Perhaps so, but she did n't know, as she never *could* read them. Plutarch went round and round a story; presented all the corners of it, told all the pretty bits of gossip he could find, instead of penetrating to its secret. So she preferred his anecdotes of Heroes to his Parallels or Essays.

I said, in surprise, how much I liked the " Morals."

" Yes," MARGARET said, " even Emerson paid the book the high compliment of calling it his tuning-key, when he was about to write."

E. P. P. said Coleridge was *her own* tuning-key, and asked Margaret if she had no such friendly instigator.

MARGARET said she could keep up no intimacy with books. She loved a book dearly for a while; but as soon as she began to look out a nice Morocco cover for her favorite, she was sure to take a disgust to it, to outgrow it. She did not mean that she outgrew the author, but that, having received all from him that he could give her, he tired her. That

had even been the case with Shakespeare !
For several years he was her very life;
then she gave him up. About two
years ago she had occasion to look into
" Hamlet," and then wished to refresh
her love, but found it impossible. It
was the same with Ovid, whose luxuriant
fancy had delighted her girlhood. She
took him up, and read a little with all
her youthful glow; but it would not last.
Friends must part, but why need we
part from our books ? She regretted her
oddity, for she lost a great solace by it.

She proceeded to contrast the Apollo
with Mercury. In Egypt, Hermes was
the experimental Deity, the Brahma.

CAROLINE STURGIS asked what the
Hermes on the door-posts of the Athenian houses meant.

MARGARET thought that he posed
there as a messenger, an opener of the
gates merely, and then spoke of several

Mercuries by Raphael. One she knew, so full of beauty and grace that it seemed a single trumpet-tone. Another all loveliness was handing the cup of life to Psyche. She wondered that such symbols as Apollo and Mercury did not inspire all young men with ardor, and make them something better than young men usually are.

WILLIAM WHITE said Apollo was too far beyond the average man to do this; but that Mercury, graceful and vivacious, would naturally attract the attention.

MARGARET asked if he would be an easier model to imitate, and then repeated her anecdote about the ugly youth who longed to be a Mercury.

WILLIAM said that if his faith had been strong enough, the transformation might have taken place.

Query — what is meant by strong *enough?*

MARGARET spoke of the Egyptian Osiris in his relation to Hermes, and said that she did not like *him* to be confounded with the Apollo. He was in reality the Egyptian Jove.

This led me to speak of the Orphic Hymn in which Apollo is addressed as " immortal Jove."

MARGARET said she had discovered very little about Orpheus. In relation to the five points of Orphic theology, she had lately read a posthumous leaf from Goethe's Journal. The existence of a Dæmon seemed to be a favorite idea of his. He did not believe with Emerson that all things were in our own souls, but that they existed in *the original souls,* (does anybody know what that means?) and we must go out to seek them. This notion Goethe thought verified by his own experience. Goethe's works, Margaret thought, had more variety than anybody's except Shakespeare's. His powers of observation seemed to condense his genius.

WILLIAM WHITE wondered why Goethe showed such tenderness for Byron.

MARGARET said that in every important sense Byron was his very opposite; but Goethe hardly looked upon him as a responsible being. He was rather the instrument of a *higher* power. He was the exponent of his period.

SOPHIA PEABODY had been making a drawing of Crawford's Orpheus at the Athenæum. It was here brought down for me to see.

At Sophia's request, MARGARET repeated a sonnet she had written on it. She recited it wretchedly, but the sonnet was pleasant.

I spoke of Bode's Essay on the Orphic Poetry, and sympathized in his view of the spuriousness of the Hymns. They might have been signed Orpheus, however, as other things were signed Hermes, simply because they were exponents of Orphic thought.

MARGARET dilated on this Orphic thought.

I quoted Proclus in his Commentary on Plato's "Republic" as follows: —

"Mars perpetually discerns and nourishes, and constantly excites the contrarieties of the Universe, that the world may exist perfect and entire in all its parts; but requires the assistance of Venus, that he may bring order and harmony into things contrary and discordant.

"Vulcan adorns by his art the sensible universe, which he fills with certain natural impulses, powers, and proportions; but *he* requires the assistance of Venus, that he may invest material effects with beauty, and by this means secure the comeliness of the world. Venus is the source of all the harmony and analogy in the Universe, and of

the union of form with matter, connecting
and comprehending the powers of the elements. Although this Goddess ranks among
the supermundane divinities, yet her princi-
pal employment consists in beautifully illumi-
nating the order, harmony, and communion
of all mundane concerns."

I asked MARGARET if this was not
something like her own thought, — this
Venus, for example, was it not better
than that we got from Greek art?

She said it was the primal idea, but
she did not attach much importance to
chronology. Philosophy must decide the
age of a thought.

I gave her as good an abstract of
Bode's theory as I could.

WILLIAM WHITE took the drawing of
Orpheus from me, and, while speaking
of its beauty, said it always made him
angry to think of the deterioration of
the human figure. He thought it ought

to have been prevented, and that his ancestors had deprived him of his rights.

Upon this, MARGARET entered into a lively disquisition upon masculine beauty. She said the best specimens of it she had ever seen were a Southern oddity named Hutchinson and some Cambridge students who came from Virginia.

We lost a finer talk to-night through the inclemency of the weather. WHEELER was to have come with a great stock of information. Had he done so, I need not have quoted Bode or Proclus.

CAROLINE W. HEALEY.

April 23, 1841.

IX.

HERMES AND ORPHEUS.

April 29, 1841.

WE did not have a very bright talk. There were few present, and we had only the subject of last week. MARGARET did not speak at length. WHEELER had been ill, and his physician prescribed light diet of both body and mind.

Somebody spoke of Mercury sweeping the courts of the Gods, but that suggested nothing to Margaret.

SARAH SHAW had a pin, with a Mercury on it, represented as holding the head of a goat.

MARGARET had never seen anything that would explain it, and there was some dispute about it.

E. P. P. said that, according to the Orphic Hymn, Mercury sought the love of Dryope under the form of a goat. Pan was the fruit of that amour. In this form also he wooed Diana.

We wandered from our subject a little, to hear MR. MACK talk about the Gorgons. He thought they stood for the three sides of human nature. Medusa, the chief care-taker, the body, was the only one not immortal, and the only one beautiful. Stheno and Euryale, wide-extended force and wide-extended scope, represented spirit and intellect, essentially immortal. The changing of Medusa's curls (or elements of strength) into serpents represented the fall. It was not the Gorgons who had but one eye and one tooth between them, but three sister guardians, whom Perseus was compelled to destroy before he could reach Medusa.

MR. MACK did not tell us why human

nature so divided had a certain petrify-
ing power!

E. P. P. thought the intellect, not the
body, was the care-taker. Mr. Mack tried
in vain to explain, owing, I think, to his
German misconception of words. Certainly the five senses are the *providers*,
which was what he must have meant.

Margaret liked his theory, because
there was a place in it for sin! She
disliked failure. Perhaps we all had perceived her attachment to evil! Not that
she wished men to fall into it, but it must
be accepted as one means of final good.

The only copies of Bode belong to
Edward Everett and Theodore Parker.
Neither is at this moment to be had.
The talk turned on the age of the
Orphic idea.

The Orphic Hymns, Wheeler said,
were merely hymns of initiation into the
Orphic mysteries. They were altered by
every successive priesthood, and finally

by the Christian Platonists. Those now remaining were undoubtedly their work. Perhaps the ancient formulas were still hidden in them. We know the beautiful story of Orpheus. If he indeed represents many, yet all that has been said of him is also true of one.

MR. MACK declared that Eurydice represented the true faith! She was killed by an envenomed serpent, which might possibly stand for an enraged priesthood!

I got a little impatient here, and said I did not care to know about the Hymns; but the Orphic idea, which made Scaliger speak of the Hymns as the " Liturgy of Satan," — how old was that?

MARGARET could not guess why he called them so.

CHARLES WHEELER said that, since they made a heathen worship attractive, perhaps he fancied them a device of the Evil One!

Too great a compliment to Scaliger, I thought.

MARGARET had no objection to Orpheus as crowning an age; she liked that multitudes should produce one.

CHARLES WHEELER said that Carlyle had spoken of Orpheus as standing in such a relation to the Greeks as Odin bore to the Scandinavians.

MARGARET said at this point (I don't see with what pertinency) that Carlyle displeased her by making so much of mere men.

JAMES CLARKE quoted Milton, speaking of himself among the revellers of the Stuart Court, as like Orpheus among the Bacchanals.

I said that Bode placed Homer in the tenth century before Christ, and Orpheus in the age just preceding, say the thirteenth century before.

MR. MACK thought all that mere conjecture.

I told him it made a good deal of difference to me whether the Orphic Mythology came before or after that of Homer. Had man grown out of the noble and into the base idea? Was all our knowledge only memory? Had the Orphic fancies no beauty till the Platonic Christians shaped them?

MARGARET responded to what I said, that she did not like a mind always looking back.

E. P. P. said there was a great deal of consolation in it. Memory was prophecy. She did n't like such a mind, but since she happened to have it she wanted support for it.

MR. MACK said all history offered such support.

CHARLES WHEELER did n't like to believe it, but felt that he must. He spoke of the Golden Age.

MARGARET said every nation looked

back to this; but, after all, it was only
the ideal. The past was a curtain on
which they embroidered their pictures
of the present.

WILLIAM WHITE said that all great
men looked to the appreciation of the
future. We are too near to the present.

MARGARET agreed.

E. P. P. said, all the science of Europe
could not offer anything like the old
Egyptian lore.

MARGARET said the moderns needed
the assistance of a despotic government.

CHARLES WHEELER spoke of the monuments in Central America; but before
he could utter what was in his mind,
MARGARET interrupted, saying that all
the greatness of the Mexicans only suf-
ficed to show their littleness. We might
have lost in grandeur and piety, but
we had gained in a thousand tag-rag
ways.

Mrs. Farrar whispered to me, "Write that down!" and I have done it.

Charles Wheeler said that late discoveries proved that there was a complete knowledge of electricity among the ancients. There were lightning-rods on the temple at Jerusalem, and they are described by Josephus, who however does not know what they are.

Margaret and I clung to the " tag-rag " gain.

Charles Wheeler agreed with me in thinking the Orphic Hymns of very late origin.

Margaret could not see the use of creating a race of giants to prepare the earth for pygmies! If these must exist, why not in some other sphere? She referred to the beautiful Persian fable. The *first* was God, of course; since man may always revert to Him, what matter about the giants?

I said that primitive ages were supposed to be innocent rather than great.

MARGARET said the Persian fable bore to the same point as the Vishnu and Brahma. It was antagonism that produced all things. The universe at first was one Conscious Being, — "I am;" no word, no darkness, no light. This Conscious Being needed to know itself, and it passed into darkness and light and a third being, — the Mediator between the two. This Trinity produced ideals, — men, animals, things; and after a period of twelve thousand years all return again into the One, who has gained by the phenomena only a multiplied consciousness.

"Were they *merged?*" asked CHARLES WHEELER.

MARGARET said, "No! once created, they could not lose identity."

C. W. HEALEY.

April 30, 1841.

X.

BACCHUS AND THE DEMIGODS.

May 6, 1841.

FEW present. Our last talk, and we were all dull. For my part, Bacchus does not inspire me, and I was sad because it was the last time that I should see Margaret. She does not love me; I could not venture to follow her into her own home, and I love her so much! Her life hangs on a thread. Her face is full of the marks of pain. Young as I am, I feel old when I look at her.

MARGARET spoke of Hercules as representing the course of the solar year. The three apples were the three seasons of four months each into which the ancients divided it. The twelve labors were the twelve signs

E. P. P. accepted this, and spoke of Bryant's book, which Margaret did not like.

MARGARET said Bryant forced every fact to be a point in a case. Bending each to his theory, he falsified it. She wished English people would be content, like the wiser Germans, to amass classified facts on which original minds could act. She liked to see the Germans so content to throw their gifts upon the pile to go down to posterity, though the pile might carry no record of the collectors. She spoke of Kreitzer, whose book she was now reading, who coolly told his readers that he should not classify a second edition afresh, for his French translator had done it well enough, and if readers were not satisfied with his own work, they must have recourse to the translation. This she thought was as it ought to be.

JAMES CLARKE said it always vexed him to hear ignorant people speak of Hercules as if he were a God, and of Apollo and Jupiter as if they might at some time have been men.

MARGARET said, Yes, the distinction between Gods and Demigods was that the former were the creations of pure spontaneity, and the latter actually existent personages, about whose heroic characters and lives all congenial stories clustered.

J. F. C. did not like the statues of Hercules; the brawny figure was not to his taste.

MARGARET thought it majestic. She said he belonged properly to Thessaly, and was identified with its scenery. She told several little stories about him. That of his sailing round the rock of

Prometheus, in a golden cup borrowed of Jupiter, was the least known. She told the story from Ovid, the glowing account of his death, of the recognition by delighted Jove. She said Wordsworth's "Tour in Greece" gave her great materials for thought.

Then she turned to Bacchus.

To show in what manner she supposed Bacchus to be the *answer* or complement to Apollo, she mentioned the statement of some late critic upon the relation of Ceres and Persephone to each other.

Persephone was the hidden energy, the vestal fire, vivifying the universe. Ceres was the productive faculty, external, bounteous. They were two phases of one thing. It was the same with Apollo and Bacchus. Apollo was the vivifying power of the sun; its genial glow stirred the earth, and its noblest product, the grape, responded.

She spoke of the Bacchanalian festivals, of the spiritual character attributed to them by Euripides, showing that originally they were something more than gross orgies.

Mrs. Clarke (Ann Wilby) said that they licensed the wildest drunkenness in Athens.

I said that was at a later time than Euripides undertook to picture. Were they identical with the Orphic? Did Orpheus really bring them from Egypt?

Margaret would accept that for a *beginning.*

E. P. P. thought that next winter we might have a talk about Roman Mythology.

Margaret liked the idea, and James Clarke seemed to accept it for the whole party. He said that he had never felt any interest in the Greek stories, until

Margaret had made them the subject of conversation.

E. P. P. said she had felt excessively ashamed all through that she knew so little.

MARGARET said no one need to feel so. It was a subject that might exhaust any preparation. Still, she wished we *would* study! She had herself enjoyed great advantages. Nobody's explanations had ever perplexed her brain. She had been placed in a garden, with a great pile of books before her. She began to read Latin before she read English. For a time these deities were real to her, and she prayed: "O God! if thou art Jupiter!" etc.

JAMES CLARKE said he remembered her once telling him that she prayed to Bacchus for a bunch of grapes!

MARGARET smiled, and said that when she was first old enough to think about

Christianity, she cried out for her dear old Greek gods. Its spirituality seemed nakedness. She could not and would not receive it. It was a long while before she saw its deeper meaning.

CAROLINE W. HEALEY.

May 7, 1841.